# Meeting the
# Messiah

# MEETING THE MESSIAH

Donald J. Shelby

The Upper Room
Nashville, Tennessee

The scripture quotations not otherwise identified are from the Revised
Standard Version of the Bible, copyrighted 1946, 1952 and © 1971 by
the Division of Christian Education, National Council of Churches of
Christ in the United States of America, and are used by permission.

Material by Harry Pritchett appearing on pages 23-26 is reprinted by
permission, *The St. Luke's Journal of Theology,* the School of Theology, The University of the South, Sewanee, Tennessee 37375. Copyright 1976.

On page 61 is the poem "Palm Sunday and Monday" from *OVER THE
SEA, THE SKY* by Edwin McNeill Poteat. Copyright, 1945, by Harper
& Row, Publishers, Inc. Reprinted by permission of the publisher.

*Cover photo by John Netherton*
*Book design by Jim Moore*

First Printing, January, 1980 (8)
Second Printing, December, 1981 (8)
Third Printing, March, 1987 (3)
Fourth Printing, March, 1989 (3)
Fifth Printing, July, 1990 (5)
Sixth Printing, August, 1991 (3)
Seventh Printing, April, 1993 (2.5)
Library of Congress Catalog Card Number: 79-57363
ISBN 0-8358-0398-8
Printed in the United States of America

*For Jean, Dana, and Darla who go many first and second miles and give special meaning to my days.*

# Contents

# Foreword

Having experienced some harrowing brushes with death which had reawakened his desire for a greater faith, a young Navy pilot came to me with questions and yearnings. He wanted to meet Jesus in a personal encounter, for his acquaintance was only secondhand from listening to and reading the testimony of others. In unhurried moments of conversation, we talked about how one meets the Messiah and where.

I suggested there are certain "openings" before which we intentionally place ourselves and through which God's Spirit in Christ reaches us. One writer calls them "grooves of grace." They include daily prayer and meditation; reading the Bible devotionally and with careful study; taking risks of faith; sharing with other believers in a small discussion/growth group; getting involved in a cause which serves the needs of others; stretching the mind with a good book of substance; participating in a spiritual life retreat; practicing the disciplines of fasting and tithing; and using special seasons such as Lent for concentrated study and consciousness-raising experiences.

I also told him about meeting the Messiah in my own life. Do you remember when you first met him? My first decisive encounter remains as fresh today as if it were happening now as I write this, but that moment was only the beginning, as are all such moments. Across twenty years in the pastoral ministry I have met the Messiah many times—or more correctly, he has met and found me. The narrative which follows centers on such intersections in my own life and the lives of others.

Emil Brunner averred that truth is encounter. Those who claim the revelation and promise in Jesus Christ find it so. Along some Emmaus road, in some personal "either/or" wilderness, in dark intervals of uncertainty and loneliness, when we are trudging through a daily routine, when we are reaching out to help a stranger in need, or when joy in us is like the shiver of trees at daybreak—suddenly we are joined by Another. As he goes with us where we have to go, or as we do what we know he wants us to do, we realize who he is. With Andrew of old we declare, "We have found the Messiah!" (John 1:41) Or with the apostle Paul, we sing the glory of it, "Last of all, as to one untimely born, he appeared also to me" (1 Cor. 15:8). Once we meet him we are never alone again, no matter how faith ebbs and flows or awareness comes and goes. Once he comes to meet us and we walk on together, no night is ever too long, and no contradiction is ever that final.

Tucked away in the closing lines of Paul's hymn on love in chapter 13 of First Corinthians is a promise that has been pivotal for me. "Now I know in part; then I shall understand fully, *even as I have been fully understood*" (v. 12, italics mine). There is much we do not know about the little that we do know, and there are mysteries we shall never understand. It matters not, for we are understood, and that is what we need to know for sure. "I will not leave you desolate; I will come to you" (John 14:18). And the Messiah does, and because he does we know God cares with an everlasting love and that he understands.

We may meet the Messiah this Lenten season. He may meet us today or next week, around the corner of whatever problem we are dealing with, or at this very moment. "He who calls you is faithful, and he will do it" (1 Thess. 5:14).

This book is designed to be used during Lent in personal meditation and/or by small discussion and sharing groups. Questions for reflection and study are included, and they may be used as "starters" for dialogue and conversation in small groups. Chapter one serves as an introduction. There follow eight chapters, two through nine, one of which can be used each week. Chapter seven has a Palm Sunday theme and chapter eight focuses on Easter's celebration of Christ's resurrection. The concluding chapter bids us become agents of the Resurrection through whom others may meet the Messiah.

I am grateful to the clergy colleagues and staff with whom I have served and to the United Methodist congregations with whom I have shared the partnership of the gospel and in whose fellowship I have met the Messiah: St. Matthews in Hacienda Heights, St. Mark's in San Diego, and First Church, Santa Monica, California.

My special thanks to my secretary, Sandi Agnew, who often knows better how to say it than I do and whose enthusiasm is contagious.

DONALD J. SHELBY

# CHAPTER ONE

# When It Is Yes or No

*Read: Matthew 4:1-11; Mark 10:17-22*

Every metropolitan area now has its "traffic watch," with helicopters hovering over freeways and major thoroughfares, and radio stations advising motorists about tie-ups, accidents, and slowdowns. On a recent morning, a radio announcer in my area was updating conditions. He reported that the inbound lanes of one freeway were jammed for miles. An overturned semitrailer truck had spilled its entire load of cherry tomatoes and green peppers, making the roadway a veritable sea of relish. The reporter then advised against using any surface streets, since they were clogged to a standstill. He suggested taking two other freeways to bypass the congestion. After further checking, he indicated they were also tied up. He concluded with an exasperated sigh, "You might as well *stay* home, or turn around and *go* home!"

It is good to have alternate routes and bypasses. Wise planners always try to have ready some contingent action in case of interruption or obstacle. There are certain decisions in life, however, for which there are no options. Now-or-never moments come when our only response is either yes or no. There is a personal wilderness for each of us, a lonesome valley which, like Jesus, we must walk by ourselves because no one else can walk it for us. In his wilderness, Jesus had to choose; he had to say yes or no. He said no three times, but each no was a magnificent yes. His no to temptation was his yes of faith, his yes to vocation, his yes to obedience, his yes to God's promise and claim. He made his radical choice and encouraged others to make theirs.

Consider the young patrician who meets Jesus one day in Judea. Prosperous and prominent, a good and decent man in every sense of the word, he comes to Jesus with a sense of unfulfilled need. He asks Jesus the question of questions, "What must I do to inherit eternal life," to enter the Kingdom, to have peace of soul? (Mark 10:17) Jesus' reply is terse: "Go, sell what you have, and give to the poor, . . . and come, follow me" (Mark 10:21). With that summons, the moment is suddenly charged with crisis. The man's life is now poised in the balance. The choice is too clear, and he must decide. His face must reflect it all. Minutes pass like hours, as they do in such a vortex. Finally, the man lowers his eyes and slowly turns from Jesus to begin the long, slow retreat of saying no. He has come wanting to say yes, but the possibility which Jesus lays before him is not what he expects. He wants some options, but when there are none, he quits the quest.

I know something of what he must have felt as he walked away, for I have said no to Jesus. I have wanted an alternate route and, finding none, turned on my heel in retreat. In those pivotal wilderness moments, I have discovered what the Judean patrician must also have realized.

Such crisis moments of decision force us to scrutinize our absolutes. Absolutes are those things in life we hold irrevocable, those things we are convinced we cannot live without, those things we believe are imperative for happiness and security. Absolutes are those things upon which we base our self-esteem and by which we measure our worth and evaluate all experience. Absolutes are what give meaning to life for us.

To meet the Messiah in a yes-or-no encounter forces us to examine and to admit what we hold absolute, which is exactly what happened to the rich young ruler long ago. Jesus had—and still has—a disturbing way of putting everything into a different perspective. In his presence we cannot get by with "almost" or "maybe" or "later." A confrontation with Jesus is always a rigorous examination of the "musts" of our life. It is not unlike sifting through the ashes after a fire has destroyed our home and the possessions of a lifetime. In that aftermath we slowly relearn what we actually keep and what we value most. Or it is not unlike lying in the intensive care unit of a hospital after a massive coronary. In the silent darkness of early morning, we ask where all the hurrying and demanding, all the striving and spending bring us—at last. As a character in a recent novel observed, "Sometimes having everything is closer to having nothing than the unsucessful will ever imagine."[1]

Tony is the grandson of the founder of a vast grocery supermarket chain. He has been a rich kid all of his life. He grew up in Newport Beach and Rolling Hills, two posh areas in southern California. He graduated from college and toured the world. He was a leading long-distance swimmer and a member of the U.S. Olympic Kayak Team at Munich and Tokyo. He was unsettled, however, and the affluent lifestyle to which he was accustomed became empty and stale.

Five years ago Christ met Tony in the poor people of Tijuana, Mexico, and Tony said yes. He has been there ever since, serving the people who live in the shacks of Colonia Pedregal, one of the most impoverished districts in Tijuana. Tony had purchased a much-used bus, and he began by transporting people who needed medical help to clinics. Wherever he went, kids gathered around the bus. He learned they were hungry; some of them were without home or family, and others were left all day to fend for themselves. Tony began to feed the children on the old bus. Later he built a stone-block home, which today is known as *Hogar De Los Ninos* (The Children's Home). It is not a very fancy place, but there is ample food to eat, sufficient mattresses to sleep on, benches to sit on—and there is love, because Tony cares. For many years Tony rejected the church and was indifferent about religion. Today he is studying to be a minister.

Crisis moments of decision reveal what we hold as absolute. Meeting the Messiah, we come face to face with what we value most. The young patrician who knelt before Jesus came ready to say yes, but he said no and turned away.

He turned away because Jesus reminded him that there was only *one* absolute; namely, God, and serving in his kingdom of love. That is the only *must* in life, and all else is subordinate and of secondary importance. "One thing you lack," Jesus said to the young man. One thing remains to be done, one last decision must be made in order to find what you seek. "Go, sell all you have, give to the poor, and come, follow me!" Jesus recognized that for this man possessions had become his absolute. For others who came to Jesus, it was not possessions but status and rank. For others it was family connection, religious tradition, display of intellect and learning, or even their physical limitations which had become the commanding absolute of their lives. In each case, Jesus challenged that absolute: One thing remains to be done (for) "you shall love the Lord your God with *all* your heart, soul, mind and strength and your neighbor as yourself" (Mark 12:30-31, my paraphrase).

We cannot have it both ways. There is no alternate route. "No one can serve two masters," said Jesus, "for either he will hate the one and love the other, or he will be devoted to the one and despise the other. You cannot serve God and mammon" (Matt. 6:24). Jesus knew whereof he spoke, for in the wilderness he had declared his yes to God and his no to compro-

17

mise, expediency, and idolatry. "You shall worship
the Lord your God and him only shall you serve"
(Matt. 25:10). So with us. We cannot worship God
and at the same time idolize fame, our job, the latest
pleasure, a car, a wardrobe, a house, a college degree,
a past. We cannot at the same time live a life of caring
love and a life of indulgent self-serving. We cannot
make both possessions and persons absolutes. We
cannot have it both ways. In the words of the spiritual "Do Lord": "If you can't bear the cross, then
you can't wear the crown." There are no alternate
routes.

Two men were part of a small Lenten sharing group
in their church. They were discussing personal commitment to Christ and how we translate it into our
everyday life, our relationships, our business affairs.
One man asked, "What would happen to me if I
should undertake to carry on my business as Christ
would want me to? It might mean financial ruin."

There was a moment of silence, and then one of the
other men replied, "And what will happen if you
don't? What *kind* of ruin do you want?"

We cannot have it both ways. In our personal wilderness we will meet the Messiah. His word abides:
"One thing you lack . . . then come, follow me."
That is our summons and our promise, and it is either
a yes or no.

# CHAPTER TWO

# When We Want Proof

*"Signs" ? God*

*Read: Exodus 17:3-7; Matthew 16:1-4*

John Updike has a short story which centers around a young man who struggles with his rejection of his childhood religious faith. One night while lying in bed, he decides upon a kind of last-ditch test. He lifts his hands into the darkness about his face and begs Christ to touch them. He asks only for the faintest of contact, saying that would be enough for a lifetime. His hands wait in the air. He feels something, but he is not sure whether it is the movement of the air, the pressure of his pulse, or someone's touch.[2]

Something of that same yearning is in each of us. Often we feel that the faintest touch or the briefest vision would be enough to settle our doubts and answer our uncertainty. Ours may be a skeptical age, but our skepticism is the reverse of a deep longing. We want to know for sure.

During their desert wanderings, the Hebrews clamor at Moses again and again for a sign from God that will rally their flagging spirits and encourage them on their way. At one point in the story their canteens are empty, there is no water, and they are thirsty. Once more they press Moses, "Why did you bring us up out of Egypt, to kill us?" (Exod. 17:3) So Moses turns to God for another sign. Moses is instructed to strike a special rock on Mount Horeb. Water comes forth, and the people drink. Moses names the place *Massah* (which means "proof") and *Meribah* (which means "contention"), because of the people's demand for proof.

Have we not also had our own Massah and Meribah? We would like some sure sign, and we crave a certainty. A child asks, "Where is God?" and her mother says, "God is everywhere." The child cries out, "But I want God to be somewhere!" So do we! We want God to be now, here. We want God to prove his existence instead of leaving us with gnawing questions. We want a clue or a signal to convince the unbelievers and to corroborate our faith. We want God to make a verifiable appearance in the midst of the world's scoffing denial. Frederick Buechner imagines how it might be:

Suppose, for instance, that God were to take the great, dim river of the Milky Way as we see it from down here flowing across the night sky and were to brighten it up a little and then rearrange it so that all of a sudden one night the world would step outside and look up at the heavens and see not the usual haphazard scattering of stars but, written out in letters light years tall, the sentence: I REALLY EXIST, or GOD IS. . . . with suns and moons to dot the i's and the tails of comets to cross the t's.[3]

Why not? The scripture records how God gives signs to those who ask for them. One thinks of Gideon, who asks God to give him a special clue by wetting with dew a fleece of wool. While keeping the ground all around the fleece dry, Gideon lays the fleece on the threshing floor. It happens, but to have positive proof, Gideon reverses his request. The next morning the fleece is dry and the ground around is wet with dew (Judg. 6:36-40). Or there is Elijah in the contest on Mount Carmel with the priests of Baal. He asks for a sign, and the fire of the Lord falls from heaven to consume his sodden altar and sacrifice (1 Kings 18:30-39). It is little wonder, then, that the Pharisees pressed Jesus for a sign—not just any sign, but a "sign from heaven," they said. If he were divine, he should be able to arrange some pretty spectacular phenomena to authenticate his claim, just as the prophets did.

We are akin to the Pharisees in their demand for proof. We want God to do it big so doubt and scoffing will be silenced. Something of this craving accounts in part, I think, for the attention to and the attraction on the part of some believers to outward signs. I do not denigrate the meaning people find in such experience. However I challenge the assumption that without such outward signs, one's inward grace is suspect and one's faith is shallow. Such presumption is the lurking danger in demand for or reliance on overt signs as proof of God's presence.

The danger is encapsulated in Sinclair Lewis's banter on a public platform. He dared God to strike him dead, and when nothing happened, he said, in effect, "There! You see. There is no such God." The argument could have gone in the other direction, however. Perhaps only a God of graceful love would endure that kind of nonsense and let him go on living. Only a God who cares in ways that beggar our imaginings would listen to all our manipulative bargaining and self-justifying and keep on caring. Indeed, faith in God is less apt to proceed from signs and miracles than signs and miracles from faith in God.

There are all kinds of signs today, but *not* to prove God exists. What do overt proofs prove anyway—and for how long? The signs which God gives are not to win any debate or to cater to our intellectualism. Rather they beckon us into a relationship of trusting love. The signs do not prove God's existence, but they offer us his presence, which is what we really want and need. The signs are not given with supernatural effects which might draw a gaping crowd and make our hearts beat faster but leave those hearts untouched.

God's sign is given in the helter-skelter events of our ordinary day: the birth of a child, the work-etched hands of a grandmother laid in blessing, a teacher's contagious quest, rejection that ends in embracing, the lifting of a fallen stranger, the moral courage in someone who stands against tyranny, leaving and coming home again, keeping vigil with another through pain and dying, the last crust of bread broken and shared. His voice is not thundered from some Mount Horeb but is whispered in the interminable voice within us and pronounced in the persons we love and in their love for us. His sign is traced in the needs of human hearts and in the struggles for freedom and justice. God's presence is felt in those moments of personal truth when we say yes or no. His sign is Jesus Christ, who moves in untroubled lives with holy discontent and in troubled lives as healing peace. Jesus himself declared it would be this way: "The kingdom of God is not coming with signs to be observed; nor will they say, 'Lo, here it is!' or 'There!' for behold, the kingdom of God is in the midst of you" (Luke 17:20-21).

Harry Pritchett, Jr., describes how God gave a sign in a third-grade Sunday school class:

> Once upon a time I had a young friend named Philip. Philip lived in a nearby city, and Philip was born a mongoloid. He was a pleasant child—happy, it seemed—but increasingly aware of the difference between himself and other children.
>
> Philip went to Sunday School. And his teacher, also, was a friend of mine. My Sunday School teacher friend taught the third grade at a Methodist Church. Philip was in his class, as well as nine other 8-year-old boys and girls.
>
> My Sunday School teacher friend is a very creative teacher. Most of you know 8-year-olds. And Philip, with his differences, was not readily accepted as a member of this third-grade Sunday School class. But

my teacher friend was a good teacher, and he had helped facilitate a good group of 8-year-old children. They learned and they laughed and they played together. And they really cared about each other—even though, as you know, 8-year-olds don't say that they care about each other out loud very often. But my teacher friend could see it. He knew it. He also knew that Philip was not really a part of that group of children. Philip, of course, did not choose nor did he want to be different. He just was. And that was just the way things were.

My Sunday School teacher friend had a marvelous design for his class on the Sunday after Easter last year. You know those things that panty hose come in—the containers look like great big eggs. My friend had collected ten of these to use on that Sunday. The children loved it when he brought them into the room. Each child was to get a great big egg. It was a beautiful spring day, and the assigned task was for each child to go outside on the church grounds and to find a symbol for new life, put it in the egg (the old panty hose containers), and bring it back to the classroom. They would then mix them all up, and then all open and share their new life symbols and surprises together one by one.

Well, they did this, and it was glorious. And it was confusing. And it was wild. They ran all around, gathered their symbols, and returned to the classroom. They put all the big eggs on a table, and then my teacher friend began to open them. All the children were standing around the table.

He opened one, and there was a flower, and they ooh-ed and aah-ed.

He opened another, and there was a little butterfly.

"Beautiful," the girls all said, since it is very hard for 8-year-old boys to say "beautiful."

He opened another, and there was a rock. And as third graders will, some laughed, and some said, "That's crazy! How's a rock supposed to be like new life?" But the smart little boy whose egg they were speaking of spoke up. He said, "That's mine. And I knew all of you would get flowers, and buds, and leaves, and butterflies, and stuff like that. So I got a rock because I wanted to be different. And for me, that's new life." . . .

He [the teacher] opened the next one, and there was nothing there. The other children, as 8-year-olds will, said, "That's not fair—that's stupid!—somebody didn't do right."

About that time my teacher friend felt a tug on his shirt, and he looked down and Philip was standing beside him.

It's mine," Philip said. "It's mine." And the children said, "You don't ever do things right, Philip. There's nothing there!"

"I did so do it," Philip said. "I did do it. It's empty—*the tomb is empty!*"

The class was silent, a very full silence. And for you people who don't believe in miracles, I want to tell you that one happened that day last spring. From that time on, it was different. Philip suddenly became a part of that group of 8-year-old children. They took him in. He entered. He was set free from the tomb of his differentness.

Philip died last summer. His family had known since the time that he was born that he wouldn't live out a full life span. Many other things had been wrong with his tiny, little body. And so, late last

July, with an infection that most normal children could have quickly shrugged off, Philip died. The mystery simply enveloped him completely.

He was buried from that church. And on that day at that funeral nine 8-year-old children marched right up to that altar—not with flowers to cover over the stark reality of death. Nine 8-year-olds, with their Sunday School teacher, marched right up to that altar and laid on it an empty egg—an empty, old discarded holder of panty hose.[4]

God gives us signs which beckon us to claim his grace and live as agents of his love. He is still on the premises!

# CHAPTER THREE

# When False Expectations Fail

*Read: Genesis 12:1-9 and John 4*

A certain Taiwanese suitor wrote some seven hundred love letters proposing marriage to his girl-friend over a period of two years. His persistence finally brought results. The girl became engaged to the mailman who regularly delivered all the letters. Things do not always turn out as we expect. One of life's continuing tasks is to identify false expectations and move beyond them. Abraham faced that challenge as he lived out his response to God's call. Jesus encouraged it in the woman of Samaria, and he gives to us the same summons.

One false expectation that deludes us is that a single event will make all the difference. Many persons believe that somewhere, someday, something will happen to solve everything, and the world will finally shine for them. When we meet the right person, when we land the right job, when we lose twenty pounds, when we get a larger house, when the kids finally grow up, when we can shoot golf in the low seventies, or when we retire, then never, never again will we ask anything of life. We do, however, because no one moment is infinite, no one thing makes all the difference. In that best-seller *Passages,* Gail Sheehy describes how it happens:

> He can afford to tan it in the Caribbean on an income nearly ten times the peak of his father's earnings. . . . He can tint out the gray in his hair, tone up the doughy muscles of middlescence on the most exquisitely devised exercise tables in Manhattan, take the woman of his choice out to dinner at "21," and take back any traces of psychic discomfort to a Park Avenue psychiatrist. . . . At the age of 46, . . . he has placed near the top of the heap.
>
> "I'm near the top of the mountain that I saw as a young man, and it's not snow. It's mostly salt," he blurted out.
>
> "Most guys I talk with who are successful—whatever . . . successful is—left their personal lives way behind them. They stopped growing at age 12 or 14. . . . Professionally, they're terrific, but their personal lives are in a *mess.*[5]

No one thing makes all the difference, because no one moment is infinite. This is true of reverses as well as achievements. A shattering failure comes or some devastating loss occurs, and we believe things will never be the same, that we cannot go on. Things may never be quite the same, but life goes on, and in time we go on with it. The God-given resilience of the human spirit and the capacity to endure are amazing. What we expected to be the end—so much so that we threw up our hands and said, "Well, that's it. It's all over!"—was not the end after all. By God's grace we get up and have another go at it. The apostle Paul, out of his personal "endgames," could say, "We are afflicted in every way, but not crushed; perplexed, but not driven to despair; persecuted, but not forsaken; struck down, but not destroyed" (2 Cor. 4:8-9).

Even our commitment to Christ, which makes more difference than anything else, does not bring instant realization or total revelation. To dedicate one's life to Christ is, more than anything, to discover possibility and to be in pilgrimage. Or to put it another way, faith is traveling hopefully rather than arriving. In the words of Paul: "Not that I have already obtained this or am already perfect; but I press on to make it my own" (Phil. 3:12). Believing is only the beginning. Then we experience the ebb and flow of faith, progress and regress, fallow times, backsliding and new beginnings.

Does this mean that nothing matters, that we are forever unsettled, that we never have a place to stand, that there are no certainties? No! There are certain hours of insight, moments of transcendence, experiences of assurance when God's presence is a glory. These are not discounted or denied. However, the world does not begin or end at the boundary of our skin or mind or place in time. Today seldom hands us the same thing twice. Moreover, there is always that element of surprise. No one event, insight, or defeat is ever 100 percent definitive. No, not even death, for we live on this side of Easter, and it is always the third day. He is still on the premises!

This suggests another false expectation; namely, our world will always remain the same, and we can keep things as they are.

Two preschoolers were engrossed in television. Just as the cartoon was moving to its climax, one of the two got up and turned off the set. "Hey," demanded the other, "Wha'd you do that for?"

"'Cause," said the first, "I gotta go to the bathroom, and I don't wanna miss nothing."

We may smile at such childlike naïveté, but there are moments when all of us want to stop what is happening and stay the relentless passage of time or reverse it. Change frightens most of us. A little novelty goes a long way. Give us the familiar, the well-worn, the already "broken in." Enough of this wandering in strange territory; take us back to Haran.

We also crave a sameness in persons closest to us. When we see them changing, something akin to panic overwhelms us. Ask any parent of a new teenager! Ask the citizens of Nazareth when a young carpenter turned itinerant teacher! Ask Peter who tried to make Jesus be what he wanted him to be. Yes, we often try to keep persons from changing: "Good old Dad . . . good old Harry . . . good old Sarah. You can always count on them." By which we mean we want them always to stay the same for us. I wonder if that is why today we are overinfluenced by two sciences that deal with life as it is: sociology and psychiatry. I have no quarrel with either, but the gospel of Jesus Christ speaks of life as it might become and presents the power of God's creative and transforming love through which it happens.

Persons do change and grow, and the world does not stand still. We never know what a day may bring forth. There are contingencies we cannot predict or control which break upon us with breathtaking upheaval. Passing time alters and modifies circumstances and personalities. If we are claimed by God's grace, if we are loving and being loved, we risk being changed, and we will change.

A film was released a few years back entitled *The Subject Was Roses*. It concerned a young man who after three years in the Army returned home a different person: more mature and independent. The effect of this change on his father and mother comprised the gist of the story. They did not know how to handle it. The whole family structure cracked. Because one person changed, everyone had to change. The same thing happened in Jesus' family, so much so that his mother and brothers tried to talk him out of his mission and bring him home. Read the fourth chapter of John with your imagination wide open. You can feel the shockwaves of change that went through that Samaritan village of Sychar because the woman who met Jesus at the well was transformed. Persons grow, and change comes. The world does not stay the same.

It follows that we never finally arrive. That, too, is a false expectation for some people. They believe a day comes when we will have all the answers and all the problems will be solved. For them faith and maturity are a final outcome which you can mark on your calendars or write down in your diary. "Dear Diary: Today I became mature. Today I became sanctified. Today I finished the whole thing." That is not the way it happens. We never stop learning; we are forever becoming; we are never born enough; we are always growing and going on.

We see this in Abraham, who leaves Haran with its security and familiarity to hazard the unknown. He reaches one stopping place after another only to discover he must keep moving on. So with us. Life is forever a journey. There are way stations but few settlements or conclusions. So much that happens is but another beginning. The words of the early church underscore it: "Let us run with perseverance the race that is set before us, looking to Jesus the pioneer and perfecter of our faith. . . . Lift your drooping hands and strengthen your weak knees, and make straight paths for your feet" (Heb. 12:1b-2, 12).

To follow Christ is to be on the move in perennial adventure, on tiptoe anticipation, open to God's leading and trusting his promise. Something of this is captured in the figure of Jesus sitting beside Jacob's well and looking at Mount Gerizim, both symbols of the past, and saying to the woman of Samaria, "The water I give will become a spring of water (always fresh, lively, flowing), welling up to eternal life . . . the hour is coming and now is, when the true worshipper will worship the Father in spirit and in truth" (John 4:14b, 23, my paraphrase). This is *new*, says Jesus. It is dynamic—not a fixed and static reliance on what has been. "Break out," he says, "face the future, embrace the new, be a pilgrim and follow me." To be a Christian is, indeed, to be born again: born *again* and *again* and *again*.

A certain Army man had been a heavy drinker for thirty-five years. He had the temperament of a top sergeant long after he had become a colonel. He encountered Christ, and his whole life was changed. He was speaking once, before a group of medical men. He told them of his personality change: how he was now temperate as he had once been intemperate; considerate as he had once been severe; concerned for others as he had once been self-serving. A psychiatrist, who believed that personalities are so firmly set early in life that no one can change, protested to the colonel that at his age a person could not have such a radical transformation. "Well," replied the colonel, "at least I am under new management. I now answer to another authority—the highest and truest there is."

God is still on the premises. Christ goes before us and beckons us beyond false expectations and empty illusions to live in God's transforming and life-completing power.

# CHAPTER FOUR

# *When Feelings Are Real*

*Read: Mark 2:15-22*

When a respected theatrical producer died, the minister presiding at the funeral service invited those in attendance to join him in ringing down the curtain in what he suggested was the most appropriate way possible—with a standing ovation. So everyone at the funeral service stood, and the applause was loud and long. Different? Yes. Irreverent? Who's to say?

In Allentown, New Jersey, a cemetery caretaker, weary of gloomy funerals, left instructions in his will that two fire engines be hired for his last rites. They were. With sirens whining and lights flashing, the first carried the casket to the cemetery, and the second carried the flowers and the pallbearers. Unconventional? Yes. Irreligious? Who's to say?

Who determines, after all, what is appropriate religious behavior? Who tells us which feelings and moods are OK for Christians and which are not? I have known and been with sincere believers in a crisis as they denied and repressed their true feelings because they believed that Christians were not supposed to feel a certain way. A young woman told me how it was for her on the day of her father's funeral. She said when the family, relatives, and friends gathered after the memorial services, it was like a family reunion. People ate, talked a lot, and shared in moments of hearty laughter. She said she suddenly felt very guilty for the good time people were having because she thought everyone should be acting more solemn. But I say, "Who says so?" If we were to accept the opinion of some persons, Christians would have no feelings at all. Where did we ever get the idea that reverence must be emotionless?

To be human is to have feelings and to express them. We are rational creatures, it is true, but we are also sentient creatures with emotions. We get excited and depressed, we love and hate, we feel hostile and forgiving, we laugh and we cry. Stimuli bombard us constantly, and our affective reactions shape who we are and what we do. Genuine feelings and emotions are spontaneous, not reasoned or contrived. In fact, they defy analysis and logic. They are sometimes so difficult to understand and control that no one is ever 100 percent successful in handling them. They are so innate that when we try to deny them or repress them, we end up sick, empty, and less than human. On occasion we are tempted to set aside our emotions when the stress of life brings an ache so big it is like a rock in the stomach that does not go away. A kindergartner dropped a heavy toy on her foot and tear-fully wailed to her mother, "I wish we couldn't feel." We are human, however, and we do feel.

Therefore, when persons in the name of religion shame the natural, normal expression of feelings, the result is a sometimes cruel, often dull and jaded religion without the smell of life. Jesus would not recognize many sober Christians today in their joyless poses. Jesus embraced life with all his feelings and loved persons with his whole being—with passion and stimulation. The Gospel record makes that plain. We read how he rejoiced in the spirit (Luke 10:21), how he sighed deeply (Mark 8:12), how his spirit was troubled (John 13:21), how he was deeply moved (John 11:38), how his look revealed his anger (Mark 3:5), how he responded with immediate compassion to human need (Mark 1:40-41), how he loved and cared with openness. He could be impatient. His sense of humor was obvious (Matt. 23:24-25), as were his spontaneous ways with children. He had a good time with a variety of persons, so much so that his detractors criticized him for it. He also had darker hours when he felt the effects of frustration, disappointment, and rejection. His closest friends misunderstood him, denied him, and one betrayed him. He wept over Jerusalem, and as he moved through that final week of his earthly ministry, the whole range of human emotions emerged in him. So the writer of Hebrews said of him, "Jesus offered up prayers and supplications, with loud cries and tears" (Heb. 5:7). Yes, Jesus had the same feelings we do. To be fully human, as he was, and to come alive completely, as he did, is to embrace and to express the feelings we have.

To the guest book in a certain church was added an anonymous entry which read simply: "Thank you for a place to cry." To be human is to have feelings, to express them, and to let them enrich life.

It then follows that there are no standardized moods for Christians. Anyone who tries to establish a code of appropriate feelings for the faithful tells more than he or she knows. Each of us is different, and our commitment is forever unique. There are always both the Marys and the Marthas, the Peters and the Thomases, the Pauls and the Barnabases. How we respond to life's startling mixture of experience and how we live out our salvation cannot be organized sentiment dictated by someone else. No one can homogenize the feelings of Christians.

When some self-appointed arbiter declares that at the death of a loved one we are to dry our tears and be solemn and resigned, we can respond, "Who says so?" Or when an absurd tragedy shatters us and we are told to gather courage, grit our teeth without protest, and submit calmly to what God has ordained, we can ask, "Who says so?" Life for some Christian groups becomes so serious that any sentiment is taboo and the slightest hint of levity or hilarity is deemed unbecoming. There must be no moody states of depression, no tears, no show of anger, no carefree abandon of joy that clicks its heels and whistles.

But I say, "Who says so?" Who has the warrant to declare certain feeling states unbecoming and illegitimate? By whose authority is my emotional state deemed less than Christian or irreverent? Yes, the apostle Paul spelled out the fruits of the Spirit: "love, joy, peace, patience, kindness, goodness, faithfulness, gentleness, self-control" (Gal. 5:22-23). Yet his life did not always manifest them—nor does mine—nor does any Christian's. In truth, we open ourselves to receive the fruits of the Spirit when we are honest about our real feelings, instead of acting so holy by denying or repressing them that we cease being human.

It has become very clear to me how different persons respond with different feelings to different stress situations. I can no longer try to predict how someone will feel his or her way through a crisis. There was a time when I expected persons committed to Christ to respond with certain emotions. Now I know there is no one set of emotions for all Christians. To be sure, some feelings are more productive than others in coping with our crises. Feelings must be focused lest they become diffused and distorted. None of us, however, needs to carry guilt around or believe ourselves less Christian for the particular emotions we have.

So I say it is OK to cry at the grave of a loved one and into our pillows during sleepless nights of grief and loneliness. It is OK to get discouraged and depressed during a prolonged illness and intense pain. It is OK to shake our fist at God and scream a "Why?" when our child dies. It is OK to let our joy break forth in hilarity. The gospel of Jesus Christ assures us that God understands us, that he created us with feelings, that he knows what manner of spirit we are.

My college roommate, who is now a United Methodist clergyman in Kansas, tells of the day his father was drafted into the Army in World War II:

> We took him to the Union Station in Kansas City, and, since we had never been separated from him, our ride home was quiet and gloomy. I was the oldest, though still very young, and there were my younger brother by two years and my little sister. However, we were all old enough to try to be brave so as not to make it harder on my mother. Once we reached home, however, we ran for private corners and started crying our eyes out. Then my mother gathered us up one by one, took us all into the living room and said, "We are a family, and families cry together as well as laugh and have fun together."[6]

In Jesus Christ, God gathers us together from our private corners where we are trying to hide or deny our feelings. He reaches out and assures us that it is all right to laugh, to cry, to be scared, to be angry, to get down in the dumps, or to complain. He is still on the premises, and he understands.

## CHAPTER FIVE

# *When You Pray*

*Read: Luke 11:5-13; Philippians 4:4-7*

One of the scientists who figured prominently in our national space program had four trays on his desk. Executives usually have two trays, one marked "In" and one marked "Out." On this administrator's desk, however, were four, labeled "Frantic," "Urgent," "Pressing," and "Overdue." We are hurried and tense today. Our inner life cries out for relief and renewal. We all need stamina and resilience. What frustrates us and brings us to the breaking point is not external stress—although enough is enough—but internal pressures and spiritual emptiness. If we were more certain of our inner power, we would not be so tense and driven, so overwhelmed and fragmented. Our physical health would improve, our general outlook would be positive, and our relationships with others would be deeper and more fulfilling.

We need margins of time spent in prayer. We need time alone to link ourselves with God's whole-making and enabling power. We need reflective moments of "centering," so that God can do through us what is his nature to do and what he wants to do. We need moments of what some call "unburdening," yielding and opening ourselves to the healing process which God created within us. We need periods of rigorous self-scrutiny when we sort out our feelings, admit our desires and our fears, measure the distances between ourselves and others, and listen in the silence for the truth in our souls. Prayer is not so much telling God what he already understands but clarifying what we do not yet understand about ourselves. Prayer is recognizing what God already knows, admitting what we have tried to conceal, facing what we have avoided. Prayer is finding out where we are, why we hurt, what we need, what we must do. Often with no language but with a yearning too deep for words, we present all we are to God.

Jesus was a man of prayer, and his statements about the power of prayer are without peer in religious writing. His first disciples, wanting something of his power and poise, sought his secret and found it in his prayer life. They then asked, "Lord, teach us to pray" (Luke 11:1).

He told them: "Always pray, and do not lose heart" (Luke 18:1). His parable in Luke 18:1-8 encourages us to pray and keep on praying. Prayer is no casual exercise we do spasmodically if and when we feel like it or happen to think about it. Prayer is a discipline. All creative endeavors require arduous preparation, development, and focus. No one goes up to a thoracic surgeon and says, "I'll take over for you today," or tells the captain of a jumbo jetliner, "I've always wanted to pilot a plane. Move over, and I'll take the controls." A great pianist once remarked that if he did not practice for a month, his audience knew it; if he missed practice for a week, his critics began to notice it; and if he did not practice for a day, he knew it. Any great art or skill requires serious, sustained, and disciplined preparation.

To wake to life's wonder and cope with its ambiguities likewise require discipline and preparation. The best is being constant at prayer. Someone observed astutely: "Before you do anything at all, pray about it. And if you cannot pray about it, don't do it. And after you have done anything, give thanks to Almighty God for it, and if you cannot, don't ever do it again."[7] That is no simple exercise, but to live in these days demands more than a minimal response. An occasional prayer gasped in desperation at a border moment is not enough. In order to recognize how God calls us in this new day, to know what this moment means and what God wants us to do, we *must* pray. We pray when events make us numb and words stick in our throat. We pray when the landscape is bleak and our prayer seems only an echo in the dark. We pray when life is a shining morning and we can see forever. We pray and never cease praying.

Moreover, we must be constant, because through prayer we become vulnerable enough to admit our need. We are so anxious to stay in control and want to be self-sufficient. We do not want to get caught with our defenses down. Many persons resist admitting any need at all, because, for them, need is tantamount to weakness. For a person to reach out for help is to announce to the world he or she is a failure. To receive not only the *gift* of a single day, however, but to receive the love which makes that day meaningful and to receive God's grace which makes that love meaningful, we humble ourselves. Through prayer we take the risk of openness and become reachable. Then God's full giving begins in us.

A young friend of mine discovered it and prayed:

God, are you awake?
I wasn't sure, 'cause your eyes were closed.
I know it's your day off, so I won't ask you to get up.
But I'd like to talk to you a moment before
    tomorrow gets here.
I called you during the week, but the line seemed
    busy.
I was pretty sure it was all right to call you today,
    'cause I don't have a BIG job that
    I'm asking you to do—
    like ending a war or doing another
    six-day-thing.
But I thought that maybe, while you're resting,
I would kinda tell you that it's been a rough
    week.

Jesus also said: When you pray, be expectant! So his bold promises: ''And whatever you ask in prayer, you will receive, if you have faith" (Matt. 21:22). "If you ask anything in my name, I will do it" (John 14:14). "I tell you, whatever you ask in prayer, believe that you receive it, and you will" (Mark 11:24). Jesus placed no limitation on what God would do if persons asked and then believed enough to receive. Have faith, says Jesus, and believe ahead of the evidence. Expect miracles, and believe in your answer. Be ready for God's stunning surprises of grace, which may not coincide exactly with what we are asking for but will be more than we hoped for. We cannot set boundaries on the possible. We should never underestimate God, for, as Jesus reminds us, "All things are possible with God" (Mark 10:27).

What have we believed God for lately? Do we feel inadequate and unworthy, convinced we are a failure or a nobody? Jesus challenges us to believe God enough to stand tall and take our place in the sun. Do we suffer from needless loss of health, or are we anxious about dying? Jesus challenges us to believe God for healing and for the comfort of his near presence. Are we captive of base desires and destructive compulsions? Jesus challenges us to believe God for transformation and self-control. Are we tense with active hatred or resentment toward others, or caught up in a power struggle to dominate which alienates us from others? Jesus bids us believe God for cleansing and reconciliation. Are we reduced by inconsolable grief? Jesus invites us to believe God for joy and release. In a small chapel cut out of rock on Lookout Mountain near Fort Payne, Alabama, these words have been inscribed across the front of the chancel: "God has always been as good to me as I would let him be." When you pray, be expectant!

In his book *Down These Mean Streets,* Piri Thomas describes a poignant scene in a jail cell shared by two men. One is facing a parole hearing, and the night before it is to occur he waits until he thinks his cellmate is asleep and then gets down on his knees and in the silent darkness speaks his simple, childlike prayer, asking God to help him. He concludes: "God, maybe I won't be an angel, but I do know I'll try not to be a blank. So in Your name, and in *Cristo's* name, I ask this. Amen." He hears a small voice add an amen and looks up to see the face of the young prisoner, head on bended elbow, who then tells how he believes in God and how he now feels that God is near.

> "What's it called, *Chico,* this what we feel?" I asked softly.
>
> "It's Grace by the Power of the Holy Spirit," the kid said.
>
> I didn't ask anymore. There, in the semidarkness, I had found a new sense of awareness.[8]

God *is* that near. He is everywhere: in prison cells and in church sanctuaries, on mountaintops and in coal mines, in tenement hotels and luxury resorts, on the beach and in family kitchens, in classrooms and on freeways. He draws near in Jesus Christ to grace us with power and purpose, hope and healing. When we pray, we meet the Messiah who has come to meet us. So let us pray and keep on praying with great expectation.

## CHAPTER SIX

# *When We Walk the Sometimes Longest Mile*

*Read: Matthew 5:38-42*

Persons who live along the northern edge of Los Angeles still relive that February morning when the gentle earth of Southern California became violent and an earthquake wrenched the land. Sixty aged and sick men were buried alive when the Veteran's Hospital crashed down on their infirm bodies. There was little hope for their survival, and yet countless other men worked beyond exhaustion to reach those trapped beneath tons of shattered concrete and twisted steel. Long hours of hard work stretched into days as the workers dug through the debris in search of life. Many people said the task was futile, but the workers continued to dig and found men trapped. Each time the trapped had died. The digging went on, however. Without sleep, existing on cold sandwiches, the workers persisted, their bodies bent with fatigue, their faces covered with sweat and dust. At long last—after five days had passed—they had recovered all the missing bodies—all but one. There was no hope at all for that last missing man. No hope at all. Still the workers continued to dig. The man was found. He was alive!

Being Christian includes going the second mile. Persons who go that second mile, as those rescue workers did, command our respect and attention, for in them we sense the greatness of human kindness. Acts of sacrifice, service beyond the mere call of duty, constancy of caring that seeks no recognition or reward, and crosses taken up and carried faithfully manifest the life to which Jesus calls us.

In fact, we are who we are because somewhere in our history someone walked a second mile for or with us. It may have been a friend who, in spite of other responsibilities, kept a vigil with us through dark hours of despair. It may have been a teacher who, spending many afterschool hours, stayed with us and whose quiet inspiration made the crucial difference between our hanging on and running away. It may have been a colleague who believed in us when it seemed no one else did and encouraged us to pick up the pieces and start all over again. The world is a better place to live because ordinary persons do the extraordinary, walk the second mile, take risks, and share who they are and what they have.

As wonderful as such second miles are, the first mile is equally important, and sometimes it is the longest mile. That is why some persons would rather run the second mile than walk the first, why they prefer the excitement of an unexpected challenge to the humdrum routine of the familiar, why they involve themselves in public causes and neglect everyday loyalties and near-at-hand duties.

We must always walk the first mile before we run the second, especially at home with those who know us best. Why is it that we can act on our worst impulses and often treat those closest to us in shabby ways? Some women who are genteel in public become shrews when they walk in the front door at home. Some men will go out of their way to be considerate and supportive of clients and customers, but at home they shout at their wife, cuff the dog, strut around like some Caesar issuing imperial decrees to their kids, or pout behind the newspaper. A teen-ager can talk animatedly to a friend over the telephone one moment and the next be morose and sullen to his parents and a terror for his sister.

Despite the fact that our homes ought to be a place where we can be ourselves, express our feelings, take off our masks, and find understanding, how often we exploit those privileges. I am amazed as I realize how many examples come to mind of persons (including myself) who failed to walk this first mile. There is a particular family where the father was highly esteemed in the community. He was a dynamic civic leader and a hard worker in the church, giving countless hours in many endeavors. Almost everyone who came in contact with him held him in high regard—everyone, that is, except his own family. One of his sons became an alcoholic, his daughter suffered a serious emotional breakdown, and the other son wasted his life in contemptuous rebellion against all his father stood for. People wondered why. The father was so busy walking second miles for other people that he failed to walk the first mile in his own home. Perhaps he helped to solve someone else's problem as a substitute for facing one or two of his own. Or he might have realized that the emotional commitment and intimacy in primary family relationships require more accessibility, sense of presence, and concern than secondary relationships. In secondary relationships we can assume helping roles where we stay in control, where there is lower personal risk and fewer checks upon the integrity between what we claim and how we act, what we say and what we do.

Jesus did, indeed, command his followers to move out to the crossroads of human need and do all they could, especially for the victimized stranger who cried out for help. He said we were to walk the second mile and share our love. However, before we walk that second mile of serving others, there is a first mile to walk at home. There is a first mile of fidelity in little things, keeping promises, saying what we mean and doing what we say, listening, caring how others feel and feeling how others care, and cherishing one another.

A certain father walked that first mile—or more precisely "wheeled it." He has been confined to a wheelchair for two years after a crippling accident. Recently the man "wheeled" his wheelchair eight miles to a hospital with his sick fourteen-month-old son on his lap because he did not have enough money to take a bus or taxi, and he could not reach friends or relations for help when the child became very ill with high fever and delirium. It took the father four hours to get to the hospital. His other son, eight years old, walked beside the wheelchair to steady it. The man's hands were blistered and bleeding when he arrived at the hospital. Doctors in the emergency room treated the child's ear infection and the father's bleeding hands. The hospital staff took a quick collection and sent the three home in a taxi. One doctor said, "The father had rubbed his palms raw pushing that wheelchair, and that's got to be *remarkable*."

We must walk the first mile before we run the second, which means we do what is ours to do. When we are facing Monday's mess or the other pesky duties that are ours, it is tempting to walk some second mile rather than trudging through the first that stares us in the face. I know certain persons who are great dreamers and innovators but who do not pay their bills or honor their commitments. I know students who can lay out for you all the answers to the world's dilemmas but who never seem to complete an assignment on time. I know women who volunteer their time to cook in a soup kitchen on Skid Row who never cook a decent meal for their family.

It is easier to dream of the coming Kingdom than to do the unglamorous task in front of us. The apostle Paul and members of the early Church saw it happening, and Paul wrote to the Thessalonian Christians: "We hear that some of you are living in idleness, mere busybodies, not doing any work. Now such persons we command and exhort in the Lord Jesus Christ to do their work in quietness and to earn their own living'' (2 Thess. 3:11-12). That is advice not easily accepted, however. We would much rather save the world than mop the floor, do the garbage detail, complete the report, hoe the weeds, settle the differences with our next-door neighbor. It is much easier to cross the street to lend a helping hand than to work at correcting our own problems. Total commitment which takes us down the second and third mile also involves the sometimes weary, unexciting first mile when we do what duty we have to do.

Before the diploma and the venture to improve the world, the first mile of assignments, exams, and tedious hours of study. Before the sharing of love with those who have none, the first miles of bills to be paid, diapers to be washed, deadlines to meet, illnesses to go through, reversals to endure. Before going out with banners flying to herald the Kingdom, the first mile of putting money in the collection plate, being on duty Sunday after Sunday in a classroom, getting on our knees to pray when we do not feel like it, the daily study of the Bible and listening to God's Word. Always that sometimes longest mile of doing the thing in front of us that must be done when we would rather be involved in exciting Kingdom enterprises.

Charles Ives, that unique and creative American composer at the turn of the century, wrote a simple and beautiful tribute to the fervency of his ''Aunt Sarah'':

. . . who scrubbed her life away for her brother's ten orphans, the fervency with which this woman, after a fourteen-hour work day on the farm, would hitch up and drive five miles through the mud and rain to "prayer meetin'," her one articulate outlet for the fullness of her unselfish soul.[9]

"If any one forces you to go one mile, go with him two miles" (Matt. 5:41). Being a Christian includes going the second mile; but before we run the second mile, we must walk the first, especially at home with those who know us best, and also by doing what must be done. As we walk that sometimes longest first mile, we shall, like "Aunt Sarah," meet the Messiah who promised: "He who is faithful in a very little is faithful also in much" (Luke 16:10).

# CHAPTER SEVEN

# When Loneliness Does Not Go Away

*Read: Luke 19:28-41*

It is what one writer described as "feeling like a cuckoo in a nest of swallows."

A young professional man put it this way: "You want to put your head on someone's lap and feel a closeness that is not physical or mental but spiritual."

A woman in her middle years confessed: "There have been many times when I felt it so desperately that I have gone to the greeting card rack and bought for myself the card I wished someone had sent me."

One man yearns so much to have someone speak to him that he dials his telephone to hear a recorded voice say, "The time is. . . ."

We live in an age of alienation and loneliness. Some suggest it is a loneliness of soul such as never existed before. It affects young and old, rich and poor, strong and weak. Those who live alone experience it, and so do those who are surrounded by family and friends. A recent study indicated that the loneliest of persons can be married couples—people with nice homes, good jobs, money, family activities, and all the rest, but who are out of touch with each other, who have no intimacy or mutual understanding. None of us is entirely free of loneliness, and many are desperately lonely.

There is a loneliness about that first Palm Sunday. You sense and feel it in Jesus as the donkey on which he is riding clops along the sunbaked, dusty road. Amidst the shouting and singing of the crowd, the dancing, the children running and waving palm branches, and the people craning their necks to get a better look, he rides. He rides in loneliness, because he knows most of the people have no idea what is actually going on and care less. He knows that they do not know or understand. His knowing is the pain of loneliness. At the descent of the Mount of Olives, he stops, looks across the Kidron Valley at Jerusalem, now visible in panoramic view. He weeps!

There is loneliness in the crowd, too. That is why they have come to what they think is a parade, hoping something might happen to interrupt their aimlessness, hoping the entertainment will fill their inner emptiness. They have come looking for more than crowd excitement, although they may not be aware of it. They have come because they yearn for community and connection. This Jesus of Nazareth may finally be the Messiah who will improve their lot in life and give them a sense of belonging.

Two thousand years later, we still search for community and crave a sense of belonging. We want relationships that confer meaning and give purpose to life. Our loneliness is the desire to be home, to have a place, to be with persons who care and are willing to come close. Without such relationships, we live in half-worlds. The fullness of life we savor depends directly upon how other persons relate to us and we to them in reciprocal trust. The closer we are together, the more life means to us. Life abundant is to be experienced and realized in the world of real flesh-and-blood human beings who stand together, dream and talk together, face the darkness together, suffer and sing together, and stay together.

When Speaker of the House Sam Rayburn, near the end of his life, discovered just how ill he was, he surprised his colleagues in Congress by announcing that he was going home to Bonham, Texas, for medical tests and treatment. Some of them asked why he did not remain in Washington, D.C., where he could have the use of the prestigious National Institute of Health facilities and other premiere medical centers. Rayburn told them why: "Bonham is a place where people know it when you're sick and where they care when you die."[10] We crave a sense of belonging. We need each other.

Jesus also needed people. He wanted persons close in order to savor with them the simple joy of being together. In narrating Jesus' choice of disciples, Mark says, "And he appointed twelve, to be with him" (Mark 3:14). Christ's ministry was undergirded by a relationship with those twelve and with others. They not only prayed together and discussed the Kingdom, they walked and grew weary together, washed their faces and ate together, sloshed through rain together, and slept under the open sky together. Moreover, Christ's heart went out to persons who were alienated and denied a community: the lepers, the mentally disturbed and emotionally troubled, the blind, the tax collectors, and the "people of the land" (called "sinners" in the Gospels). Such persons Jesus affirmed with love, removed their stigma of rejection, released them from their self-made tyrannies, and invited them back into the community. He served notice upon persons that God needed and wanted them. They began to believe because they could feel how much he wanted them.

Yet it was a lonesome valley Jesus walked, because most people preferred their illusions and alienation to deep sharing. Jesus soon realized that to keep faith with God's purpose meant loneliness, that loneliness was the price of reaching out in love and truth and having them scorned and rejected. He once said to the disciples, "Foxes have holes, and birds of the air have nests; but the Son of man has nowhere to lay his head" (Luke 9:58). Or, in the words of John's Gospel: "He came to his own home, and his own people received him not" (1:11). He was, indeed, a man "despised and rejected . . . a man of sorrows, and acquainted with grief [and loneliness]" (Isa. 53:3).

The poet's lines are a poignant hint of Jesus' feelings:

They pluck their palm branches and hail Him as
    King,
Early on Sunday;
They spread out their garments; hosannas they sing,
Early on Sunday.

But where is the noise of their hurrying feet,
The crown they would offer, the sceptre, the seat?
Their King wanders hungry, forgot in the street,
Early on Monday.[11]

The "hoopla" of the crowd is attractive, and the
limelight gratifies the ego, but crowds are fickle, and
relationships based on momentary acclaim do not last
past sundown. When the shouting dies, the crowds
have dispersed, the streets are empty, and the door-
ways are vacant, loneliness sets in. When laughter is
only an echo, the palm branches are trampled, the
bouquets are withered, and the night wind blows
through the olive branches of Gethsemane, Palm
Sunday promises fade. Peter may cry fervently,
"Even though they all fall away, I will not" (Mark
14:29), but before long he will be found exclaiming,
"I do not know this man [Jesus] of whom you speak"
(Mark 14:71).

Jesus needed people, but not with the superficial
smiles and the curious stares of Palm Sunday. He
needed them at the Gethsemane level of fidelity, for
relationships that matter grow out of commitment
and trust. Love is more than sentiment. It is rigor and
risk. It is tough and resolute, intense and persevering.
Love is more than good feelings, moonlight and

roses, storybook romances of happiness forever after.

Love is constancy—the constancy we see in Jesus, who, "having loved his own who were in the world, he loved them to the end" (John 13:1), even when they misunderstood him, tried to dissuade him, denied him, and forsook him. Jesus never yielded or compromised the responsibilities of love. Although it meant being treated as a stranger of no address, he stayed open to God's revelation dwelling in him. He drew persons near with reverence and care, and with concern and trust he held before them a vision, waking them to God's claim. He walked with persons and by his presence encouraged them to risk greatness and forsake littleness. "You are of great worth" (Matt. 10:31, my paraphrase); "You are the light of the world" (Matt. 5:14); "As I have loved you, . . . you also love one another" (John 13:34).

There is a risk of loneliness for us when we believe in and care about persons, when we keep on believing in and caring for them. They may reject us, impugn the very love we give to them, make inordinate demands upon us, and even violate our trust. That has been, however, is now, and always will be the cost of discipleship.

A young woman, involved in the dark days of a struggle which is not yet ended, was arrested and placed in solitary confinement in an antiquated jail cell with no window and a single light bulb. Then the jailer unscrewed the light bulb and took it, leaving her in an inky blackness. Through the darkness he taunted her: "We have taken away your light. Now what will you do!"

Her answer was immediate: "You cannot take away my light. Jesus is my light!" She was not alone in the darkness. She had made friends with the Stranger of no address.

He who knew loneliness comes to us in ours. He who was forsaken does not forsake us. He is still on the premises with love.

# CHAPTER EIGHT

# When We Are Ready to Give Up

*Read: Luke 24:13-35*

Over the entrance of the campus library at a university, the following sign appeared some time back:

Due to reorganization, the basement will be on the second floor, one half of the second floor will be on the first floor, but one half will remain on the second. We suggest you ask for help.

Life is often like that. The pieces just do not fit together. So little makes sense. Why do we have to make our living by competitive triumph over others? Why do we have to maintain our sense of security by suspicion and outguessing of others. Why are the young alienated and the elderly put away?

Today I weary of fads which parade as truth, of evil and sin glamorized as good, of injustice disguised as custom. Do you? I weary of promises that are not kept, of sudden heroes who turn out to be hucksters, of experts with opinion but no answers. I weary of tyrants who swagger while the innocent suffer and the rest do nothing. I weary of deceivers being honored and truth-seekers being crucified. I weary of the wasteful who indulge themselves, while others live in want and the rest do not care. I get tired of old history which keeps repeating itself. Do you? There are days when I want to head for Emmaus, just as Cleopas and Simon did in the aftermath of Golgotha.

Where was Emmaus? It was a little village west of Jerusalem along the main road to the seacoast, but Emmaus was not so much a place as a state of mind. It could have been any place, just as long as it was far enough removed from frustration, confusion, grief, and despair. Cleopas and Simon wanted to get away from it all in order to try to forget, to sort out their feelings and somehow find a way to start over again. With leaden feet and sagging hopes, they headed west, talking together, saying it again to make it go away and retelling it to one another to ease the pain.

They had counted so much on this man, Jesus. With the others, they were so certain he was finally *the* One—the long-awaited Messiah who would redeem Israel. There was conclusive evidence: the miracles he effected, the changed lives, and his persuasive teachings. But there was more. What was it? A contagion of love, wild and unaccountable, which drew persons, scattered their fears, and restored their significance. Then suddenly a terror was unleashed with its unbelievable nightmare which engulfed him and them. Small wonder that they huddled together afterwards, too stunned for grief, uncertain and limp, their dreams in ruins. He was dead! Rumors about his tomb being empty were passed back and forth, but in their depressed mood, the stories were like an idle tale. So these two followers of Jesus, in despair, headed west to find some space, to take some time, and, they hoped, to pick up where they left off.

We know something of how they felt, for we have searched for our own Emmaus. It may have happened to us at the betrayal of someone we respect very much, or as the one we love the most rejects us and leaves us for someone else. Or it may have happened at the death of our spouse or parent. It can occur when we are terminated by a long-time employer without explanation or commendation. Illness may have confined us, with no respite from pain. Perhaps our child was stricken and hovered between life and death, and there was nothing we could do but hold her hand and just be there—beside her. It may come with advancing age which forces us to pull up the roots of a lifetime, leave our home, and accept decreasing physical vitality.

We may seek an Emmaus when our struggles to right a wrong end in utter defeat, or when the cause to which we have given a lifetime is undermined by the deceit and corruption of a trusted leader. Or it may begin when in a moral crisis we wake up to how miserable we have made our own life and the lives of others.

At such turning points and traumas of life, like those two disciples long ago, we head out to Emmaus to get away from it all, to wait it out, or to discover how to live through it.

Hitchhikers in California who stand at the entrances to freeways and along highways announce their destination with signs they hold up or attach to their suitcases or bedrolls. Some are very specific: "S.F." (San Francisco), "L.A." (Los Angeles), "UCLA" (the nearby University of California campus). Others are less exact: "Texas," "Colorado," "New York," "Florida." Yet others are even more general: "North," "East," "South on Interstate 5." One Christmas season I saw a young man who stood holding a sign which read: "Anywhere."

In a word, that is Emmaus: anywhere away from the present crisis, the pain and darkness; anywhere we can cry, ask, ache, and find a way through.

While on our way to Emmaus we may be surprised, as those two disciples were on that third day long ago. Suddenly, when we least expect it, we are aware of the presence of Another who would go with us. Later, in some ordinary moment, we see Jesus, in the miracle of our being together and his being with us. Light dispels the darkness—light of many sunrises inside of us. In the wasteland of our despair, hope and love grow again. We discover life comes on, and he comes with it and beckons us to go on. When we do, we find we can.

Once we have experienced Jesus' presence, we can never be sure where he will appear or what he will do to reach us. It is always the third day, and no one can set limits on God's power or his purpose. Never can we know for sure how he will come, what he may bring, when he will confront us into greater becoming, when he will resurrect us. Therefore, we always have hope. No depth of humiliation or contradiction is too deep for his saving persuasion or constancy of love.

One morning while I was pastor of St. Mark's United Methodist Church in San Diego, I was called into the sanctuary upon my arrival. The custodian wanted me to see a strange offering which had been placed at the very center of the altar. Closer examination revealed it to be a pair of brown corduroy trousers, a belt, a white T-shirt, a pair of tan suede boots, and a note. There were blood stains on the shirt and on the note. The note had been written on a pledge card kept in the hymnal rack of the pews. A name was written large and underlined three times. Then a plea, also underlined: "Please listen to God." On the reverse side there was an address and a telephone number. I later made a call to the number listed and reached a young man who told me he had written the note. He was nineteen and after long wandering in the wasteland of drugs, dropping out of sight, severing contact with his family, and getting involved in one mess after another, he had come home. The night before, his whole world had crumbled. There had been a fight on the streets and an almost fatal beating.

After making sure the injured victims were taken care of in the emergency room of a nearby hospital, being interrogated by the police and released, this young man came by the church, found an unlocked door, and entered the sanctuary. He said he stayed there the rest of the night, praying, crying, thinking. He asked God to forgive him and to show him a new way to go. He said all at once God's presence was so real he could almost see him. He knew he had been forgiven, and a wonderful peace, something he had never experienced before in his brief years, settled over him. He made a commitment to follow Christ. He determined to make right what he had messed up. To symbolize his new commitment, he had put on some clean clothes he had in his bedroll and left the others as a kind of offering, giving to God his former life. He said he walked out the door a new person, with a new vision and a new hope. Today he is still living out that promise in a beautiful way. I have kept the blood-stained card with its plea as a reminder. God is still on the premises with resurrection power in Jesus Christ.

Emmaus is never too far. We may head for ours with faltering steps, with a knot in our stomach, with a hurt in our heart, and with tears in our eyes. We do not go alone. He comes to meet us. It is always the third day. "The light shines in the darkness, and the darkness has not overcome it"(John 1:5)—and cannot overcome it!

# CHAPTER NINE

# When We Are Easter People

*Read: John 21:15-19; Colossians 3:12-17*

There was a conscientious wife who tried very hard to please her ultra-critical husband but failed regularly. He always seemed the most cantankerous at breakfast. If the eggs were scrambled, he wanted them poached; if they were poached, he wanted them scrambled. One morning, with what she thought was a stroke of genius, the wife poached one egg and scrambled the other and placed the plate before him. Anxiously she awaited what surely this time would be his unqualified approval. He peered down at the plate and snorted: "Can't you do anything right, woman? You've scrambled the wrong one!"

Living together as human beings is not a simple matter. Once we come together, we are immediately subject to the ambiguities, deficiencies, and contradictions compounded in every person. So it is with the church. When critics chide the church for its internal conflicts and its attention to trivia, they are right. The flaws and wormholes, the failures and pretensions are real and quite obvious. They always have been, ever since that day when Christ chose twelve unlikely candidates as disciples and later, in his resurrected glory, commissioned those disciples and the other followers to be his agents of love in the world. Whereas the New Testament writers generously called those early Christians ''saints,'' they were well aware such saints were without halos.

The church is still comprised of very human mortals who are inconsistent, who make exaggerated claims and play their little games. But paradox of paradoxes: Christ summons us with those limitations—and more—to be agents of his resurrection power and hope. ''You did not choose me, but I chose you and appointed you that you should go and bear fruit and that your fruit should abide'' (John 15:16); ''Greater works than these will . . . [you] do'' (John 14:12); ''Go therefore and make disciples of all nations'' (Matt. 28:19); ''Heal the sick, raise the dead, cleanse lepers, cast out demons'' (Matt. 10:8). Or, in the words of Paul: ''As God's chosen ones, put on compassion, kindness, lowliness, forbearing one another, forgiving one another. Above all, put on love . . . and let Christ's Word dwell richly in you'' (Col. 3:12ff., my paraphrase). We are called to be saints, who in our humanness are always saints without halos. Christ asks us to be his Easter people, to do for others what we ourselves need. He summons us to be for others what we have not yet become and to give to others what we have not yet completely received ourselves.

We are asked to be what we are not. We who follow Christ are called to offer to others what is still unrealized in us. Lessons of love and life are to be taught by us who are still learning them. Self-understanding in others is to be encouraged by us who do not yet understand ourselves. We are to witness, nurture, and admonish others in their spiritual pilgrimage while still struggling with our own. We who are sick are asked to heal others. We who are fractious and cause conflict are called by Christ to be peacemakers. We who have dark corners in our soul still unredeemed are sent out to baptize. We who need the Word ourselves are commissioned to proclaim and to preach. We who are possessed by irrational urges and baser motives are sent out to cast out demons. We are called by Jesus to do what we need, to offer what we ourselves need.

Realizing this, some of us try to act as if we are 100-percent Christians, as if we are completely sanctified and adequate. When we are dull, we try to look sharp. When we are unsure, we talk louder. If we have doubts, we become more dogmatic. If we fail or falter, we rationalize or blame someone else. If we lose control, we clamp a lid on our feelings and look very solemn. Any Christian who believes he or she is 100 percent all of the time is wearing a mask most of the time, for much, if not most, of the time we are not adequate. Our motives are sullied and our limitations plain. The apostle Paul confessed what is true for all Christians: "When I came to you, . . . I was with you in weakness and in much fear and trembling" (1 Cor. 2:1-3). And he also used an apt analogy: "We have this treasure in *earthen* vessels" (2 Cor. 4:7, italics mine). Martin Luther seconded Paul when he said: "God carves the rotten wood and rides the lame horse."

Of course! Consider those who assemble in Christ's name in any church on any given Lord's Day. Consider yourself and all fellow believers. How Christlike is our life? Do our relationships, our attitudes, our behavior and inner thoughts manifest God's love and Jesus' way? The disparity is greater than we care to admit. That is why Christ's mandate is so astounding.

The miracle is that we make a difference. Despite our duplicity and even perversity, God does use us as his agents of grace and reconciliation. He takes our awkward gestures, our vacillations, our meager faith and selfish ways, and through us he reaches others. He does not wait until we are saints with halos. He does not wait until we are perfected or sanctified to work through us. He wants us now and takes us as we are. His resurrection power in Jesus Christ works in us, and, in ways beyond our knowing, events happen and lives are changed. Simply because we are here, his creative power moves through us to touch, to save, and to move other persons. In spite of us—and yet *because* of us—Kingdom-hope is given to someone else.

That is the story of the church across twenty centuries: unlikely candidates and unwilling disciples who, by his grace, become Christ's Body, through whom and in whom God touches other lives and redeems fragments of this dark interval. What we do not have it within ourselves to do, we find ourselves doing—and we cannot explain why or how. What we have studiously avoided doing because we felt inadequate is suddenly ours to carry out, and what we thought could never happen—does!

Robert Hudnut says it in these poignant lines:

> I think of the coffin on rollers and the freshly dug dirt and the six little chairs. I think of the young woman with laughter tumulting from her lips as she talks with her husband-to-be. I think of the little boy in an oxygen tent with his teddy bear at the foot of the bed. I think of the mother smiling the smile of first mothers as she tells of the birth of her child.
>
> And then I think of myself and my being there, and of God's coming somehow out of the nowhere into the now, here and being there, too.[12]

So it has been for me as I have followed Christ into the needs of human hearts, or when I step into the pulpit, or when I walk through a no-man's-land with a husband and wife who care for and want to love each other but are estranged from each other, or when I sit beside someone who is dying and with those who are keeping the vigil. What a contradiction! To know my unresolved searchings and my sin, to know how far I fall short of being Christlike, and then to experience God using me to magnify his purpose. It is more than I can take in. He calls us to do what needs doing for us, to be in his name for others what we lack in ourselves. He asks us ''hungry beggars'' to tell others where the Living Bread is.

Jesus charged Peter on this side of Easter: "Do you love me? . . . Feed my sheep" (John 21:17). His summons is the same for his Easter people today. That is where we come in. He is still on the premises and would go with us where he calls us to go.

# *Chapter 1*

1. Paraphrase into contemporary situations the three temptations which Jesus faced in the wilderness (Matt. 4:1-11), and discuss how the believers in Christ, whom you know, respond to such situations. Then consider how you yourself respond.

2. Make a list of "musts" in your life and rank them according to the priority you think they hold for you.

3. Reflect on one "now or never" moment in your life and share it with the group, also describing the changes in your life which followed.

4. If we were living our life with the priorities and

values which Christ lived out, what would be the most radical change we would have to make?

5. After thoughtful consideration and prayerful scrutiny, the "one thing I lack" for a *total* commitment to Christ and the Kingdom is _____

_____.

# Chapter 2

1. Have you ever "laid down a fleece," as Gideon did, asking God for a sign? If you are willing, share with the group what it was and also what happened in response.

2. Why did the Israelites want proof, and why do we want overt signs today?

3. "Faith in God is less apt to proceed from signs and miracles than signs and miracles from faith in God." What do you think this statement means?

4. What was the "sign" given in the third-grade Sunday school class experience with Philip?

5. List and discuss some clear signs you believe God is giving to us now.

# Chapter 3

1. What expectations might Abraham and his party have had as they left Haran? Project yourself into that situation and "feel" what they were thinking as they departed for an unknown destination.

2. What expectations might the following persons have had in the encounter between Jesus and the woman of Samaria?
   - the woman—
   - the disciples—
   - the townspeople—
   - Jesus—

3. Why is it that when one person in a circle of

personal intimacy changes, all persons in that same circle must change?

4. If the Gospel promise bids us never to give up or write someone off as hopeless, why can't we?

5. Share in the group two or three expectations you have about:
   - God—
   - Jesus—
   - Other persons—
   - Death—

   Let the group identify any that they see as false.

# Chapter 4

1. Why were the Pharisees and John the Baptist's disciples so critical of Jesus in Mark 2:15-22? With whom do you identify most—the critics or the criticized?

2. What emotion do you have the most difficulty handling? Share in a smaller group of two or three what it is and why you think it is difficult for you.

3. Have you ever observed feelings or emotional expressions that for you were inappropriate in some church activity? What? Why?

4. Complete the following and share some of the

responses in smaller groups of two or three:

A. When people first meet me, they_____

B. When people remain silent, I feel_____

C. When someone does all the talking, I_____

D. I feel withdrawn when_____

E. In a group I am most afraid of_____

F. When someone feels hurt, I_____

G. I am hurt most easily when_____

H. I feel loneliest in a group when_____

I.  Those who really know me think I am_____

J.  I trust those who_____

K. I am saddest when_____

L. I feel closest to others when_____

M. People like me most when I_____

N. Love is_____

O. I feel loved most when_____

P. If I could do it all over again_____

Q. My greatest strength is_____

R. I like myself best when_____

S. Being me is like_____

T. God and I are like_____

## FOR REFLECTION
## AND STUDY

# *Chapter 5*

1. What requests did you include in your prayers this past week? If God knows what we need, as the Bible says, why do we have to ask, as Jesus suggests in Luke 11:5-13?

2. Share with the group your prayer life pattern:
   A. When do you pray?
   B. Where do you pray?
   C. What bodily position do you assume?
   D. Do you use helps? (books, music, Bible reading)
   E. Do you use words all the time?
   F. How do you pray for other persons and their problems?

3. Discuss and share the group's individual response to these questions:

   A. The answer I need to believe God most for in my prayers is_____

   _____

   B. The biggest personal obstacle I need to face honestly in my prayer life which affects adversely my happiness and my relationships is

   _____

   C. The answer to prayer about which I rejoice the most is_____

   _____

4. What do you feel when prayers are unanswered? What thoughts do you have about the unheeded requests?

5. Does prayer allay your worries as Paul suggests in Philippians 4:4-7? How?

# *Chapter 6*

1. Locate and discuss other teachings of Jesus which you think are corollaries of His word in Matthew 5:38-42 (cf. Matthew 7:13-14, 21-23; Mark 8:34-37; Luke 6:43-45).

2. Share with the group examples of walking the "first mile":
   - at home—
   - with friends—
   - at work or in your profession—
   - in church—

3. Why do our primary relations reveal so clearly the integrity or lack of it between what we say we

believe and how we relate, what we claim and how we live?

4. Share a personal moment when you met the Messiah as you walked a "first" mile or a "second" mile. Along which mile do we usually expect to have the deeper spiritual experience?

# Chapter 7

1. Where does the author say loneliness emerged on the first Palm Sunday? Why there?

2. Discuss and share the reasons why people are so alienated and separated today.

3. Share in a smaller group of two or three the loneliest time in your life and how you moved through and beyond the feelings.

4. List and discuss ways in which we can help relieve or resolve the loneliness of others. How did Jesus remove the loneliness of others?

5. Why is there a risk of loneliness when we are faithful disciples of Christ?

## FOR REFLECTION
## AND STUDY

# *Chapter 8*

1. Of the many dilemmas and contradictions in our world today, what disturbs you most and makes you feel helpless or without much hope?

2. Are there "growing edges" or "circles of Light" which you perceive in our world? Share them with the group and the evidence which convinces you.

3. When did Simon and Cleopas finally recognize the resurrected Lord on the walk to Emmaus?

4. In a smaller group of two or three, share that personal experience when you came closest to "giving up." What was the "turning point" in that experience which gave you hope?

5. Locate three other biblical passages which declare the resurrection hope, and discuss their meaning for you.

# Chapter 9

1. In the post-Resurrection dialogue between Peter and Jesus, Jesus makes it clear that the surest evidence of our love for him is what? Discuss the practical application of his summons for us today.

2. What is most difficult for you in being a faithful witness for Christ and living out his expectations?

3. Share with the group one experience when you perceived that you were being an agent of God's saving power in Christ for someone else. Do you remember how you felt? When did you fully realize what was happening?

4. Discuss how we can become more available and more effective in our discipleship. What suggestions or discoveries would you share from your own spiritual adventure to help a new believer in his or her adventures?

# Notes

1. John Fowles, *Daniel Martin* (Boston: Little Brown, 1977), p. 420.

2. John Updike, *Pigeon Feathers and Other Stories* (New York: Knopf, 1962), p. 128.

3. Frederick Buechner, *The Magnificent Defeat* (New York: Seabury, 1979), p. 44-45.

4. Harry Pritchett, Jr., "The Story of Philip," in *St. Luke's Journal of Theology* 19:3 (June 1976): 210-11.

5. Gail Sheehy, *Passages* (New York: Dutton, 1976) pp. 172-73.

6. From an unpublished sermon by Ronald Sundbye. Used by permission.

7. Michael Allen, *This Time/This Place* (New York: Bobbs-Merrill, 1971) p. 122.

8. Piri Thomas, *Down These Mean Streets* (New York: Vintage, 1974), pp. 339-40.

9. Charles Ives, *Essays before a Sonata, the Majority, and Other Writings,* ed. Howard Boatwright (New York: Norton, 1979), pp. 80-81.

10. Alfred Steinberg, *Sam Rayburn a Biography* (New York: Hawthorn, 1975) p. 344

11. Edwin McNeill Poteat, "Palm Sunday and Monday," *Over the Sea, the Sky* (New York: Harper & Brothers, 1945), p. 182.

12. Robert K. Hudnut, *Surprised by God* (New York: Association, 1967), p. 127.